THE DEFENSE OF KNOXVILLE

by

Orlando M. Poe
Brevet Brigadier-General, U.S.A.

THE NORTH-WESTERN BASTION OF FORT SANDERS, SHOWING THE GROUND OVER WHICH THE CONFEDERATES CHARGED. FROM A PHOTOGRAPH.

A reproduction of an article published in 1886
as part of The Century Magazine's
Battles and Leaders of the Civil War Series

This version by Charles A. Reeves, Jr.
June, 2003

Charles A. Reeves, Jr.
Technical Illustration & Publishing
Specializing in Cartography and Genealogy

10812 Dineen Drive   (865) 966-5768
Knoxville, Tennessee 37934-1809
e-mail: reevesca@tds.net
Home Page: http://www.ReevesMaps.com

CONFEDERATE ASSAULT ON FORT SANDERS.

THE DEFENSE OF KNOXVILLE.

BY ORLANDO M. POE, BREVET BRIGADIER-GENERAL, U. S. A.

IT was determined by the Federal authorities to make strenuous efforts during the summer of 1863 to effect permanent lodgments in east Tennessee, both at Chattanooga and Knoxville, not only for the purpose of interrupting railway communication by that route, ǀ but to afford relief to a section where Union sentiments were known to exist to a very considerable extent. It was accordingly arranged that Rosecrans should move from Murfreesboro' against Bragg, while a force should be organized in central Kentucky to move toward Knoxville in coöperation. The latter movement was intrusted to General Burnside, who occupied Knoxville on the 2d of September, 1863, with part of the Twenty-third Corps, and on the 9th received the surrender of the Confederate force under General John W. Frazer at Cumberland Gap.

The greater portion of General Burnside's force was now expected to move down the Valley of the Tennessee to a connection (possibly a junction) with Rosecrans, then at Chattanooga or its vicinity. This involved leaving Knoxville to be held by a small force, and rendered it necessary to fortify the place. Accordingly, as chief engineer, I was instructed to arrange for a garrison of 600 men, intended only to hold the place against a cavalry "dash."

During the enemy's occupation of Knoxville, a very small beginning had been made toward the erection of earth-works. An insignificant line had been thrown up on the hill north-west of the college, and a slight epaulement

ǀ At the beginning of 1863 the Confederates had two lines of railway communication between their eastern and western forces: one by the coast-wise system to Savannah or Augusta, and thence southward or westward; the other by way of Lynchburgh, Knoxville, and Chattanooga, where it branched toward Memphis and Atlanta. [See also p. 746.]—O. M. P.

on the bluff overlooking the railway station. Neither of these was of use in the construction of our works. The plans for two works were submitted,— one, afterward known as Fort Sanders, on the site of the imperfect work first mentioned; and the other, afterward known as Fort Huntington Smith, on Temperance Hill in East Knoxville. These plans were approved by General Burnside, and work was at once begun by the engineer battalion of the Twenty-third Corps and a small force of negroes, but progressed slowly on account of the difficulty of getting suitable materials. The forts were not entirely completed until after the siege of Knoxville. Meanwhile our lines were extended down the valley toward Chattanooga. By the 18th of September, a battalion of cavalry in the extreme advance reached Cleveland, and the prospect for a junction was good until Chickamauga put an end to further movements in that direction, and Sweetwater became our outpost.

Early in October a force of the enemy under General John S. Williams, coming from the eastward, moved down the railroad to the vicinity of Bull's Gap, and pressed heavily upon our forces in that quarter. With such troops as could readily be concentrated, General Burnside attacked them at Blue Springs on the 10th and drove them well back toward Bristol.

On the 22d of October our outpost at Sweetwater and our reserve at Philadelphia were attacked successfully. Subsequent operations and reconnoissances resulted in the determination to abandon temporarily the Valley of the Tennessee south of Loudon. The troops were all withdrawn and the pontoon-bridge was transferred from Loudon to Knoxville, where General Sanders's cavalry command crossed it to the south side of the river, on the 1st of November. The abandonment of Loudon had in view the occupation of a stronger position on the northern bank of the river from Kingston to Lenoir's, where a pontoon-bridge was to be thrown across the Holston and the line prolonged by the right bank of the Little Tennessee.

On the 13th of November it was ascertained that the enemy had constructed a pontoon-bridge at Huff's Ferry, near Loudon, and were crossing in force to the northern bank of the Tennessee. At the same time General Wheeler, with nearly the whole of his four brigades of cavalry, made a rapid night march and crossed the Little Tennessee with a view to cutting off Sanders's command and occupying the heights opposite Knoxville; or, as stated by Longstreet, "failing in this, to threaten the enemy at Knoxville so as to prevent his concentrating against us before we reached Knoxville." Wheeler was foiled in this attempt, and soon withdrew to the north bank of the river, which he crossed at Louisville. He rejoined Longstreet on the 17th of November, after the latter had fought the battle of Campbell's Station.

Upon learning of Longstreet's movement, General Burnside took personal command of the troops available to oppose him. The operations of our forces during the next few days had for their object to delay the advance of the enemy to enable us to get our trains into Knoxville, and to forward the defensive works at that place, where it had been determined to make a stand.

Longstreet advanced from Loudon in two columns, McLaws's division taking the left road, leading to Campbell's Station, and Hood's division (commanded by Jenkins), the one to the right, following the line of the railroad to Lenoir's. The latter soon came in contact with the Federal skirmishers and drove them slowly back, but failed to reach Lenoir's that day. Every effort was made during the night to ascertain Burnside's movements, but his bold and vigilant rear-guard succeeded in completely concealing them. By daybreak the whole force was on the road, and when the Confederates advanced they found Lenoir's deserted.

The road upon which Burnside was moving, followed by Jenkins, intersects that along which McLaws was advancing, about a mile south-west of Campbell's Station. It was therefore essential to the safety of his train, if not of his entire command, that Burnside should reach the junction before McLaws. Just before daylight on the 16th of November, Hartranft's division took the advance of Burnside's column from Lenoir's and pushed forward as rapidly as the roads permitted, followed by the trains and by the other troops. McLaws, with full knowledge of the importance of seizing the intersection of the roads, was making every endeavor to get possession before the arrival of Burnside. He was opposed by a small force, but his march, like Hartranft's, was impeded by the mud resulting from heavy rains. It thus became a race for the position. Hartranft won by perhaps half an hour, and, turning west on the Kingston road, quickly deployed his division in such manner as to confront McLaws, and at the same time cover the Loudon road along which our trains were moving.

During the movement from Lenoir's, Burnside's rear-guard, composed of Colonel William Humphrey's brigade, had several sharp encounters with Jenkins's advance, in which Humphrey handled his forces so well as to excite the admiration of both friends and foes, always standing long enough, but never too long.

Scarcely had Hartranft's dispositions been made when McLaws appeared and attacked, but Hartranft steadfastly held his ground until the remainder of our troops and all our trains had safely passed. The trains continued on the road to Knoxville, while the troops were formed in line of battle about half a mile beyond the junction, with Ferrero's division on the right, and White's in prolongation to the left, whereupon Hartranft withdrew from his advanced position and took his place in line on the left of White. A small cavalry force scouted the roads on each flank of the line. About noon Longstreet unsuccessfully attacked our right, and afterward our left center. Later, taking advantage of a wooded ridge to conceal the march, he attempted to turn our left flank with three brigades of Jenkins's division, but our scouts soon discovered and reported the movement. Burnside had determined to retire to a new position about two-thirds of a mile to his rear, and this development but slightly hastened his withdrawal from the first line. The difficult and hazardous undertaking was successfully accomplished in the face of the enemy. All who saw it say that the troops moved with the greatest coolness, deliberation, and precision under a heavy and continuous fire.

McLaws's division promptly advanced to attack the new position, while Jenkins continued his turning movement, but the difficulties of the ground delayed him until nightfall and stopped his further progress. McLaws attacked and failed to make an impression, and at the close of the action Burnside remained in possession of his own ground until after dark, and then continued his movement to Knoxville, the head of his column appearing there about daybreak next morning, November 17th. He had gained his object and therefore was fairly entitled to claim a victory.

Burnside placed his whole loss in this important affair of Campbell's Station at about 300. Jenkins reported his as 174. It is probable that the losses on both sides, including McLaws's, were about equal.

During the fight Burnside had instructed me to select lines of defense around Knoxville and have everything prepared to put the troops into position as fast as they should arrive. I was well acquainted with the ground, and but little further examination was necessary to enable me to designate, in writing, the proposed location of each organization.

The topographical features of the vicinity of Knoxville give that place decided strength as a military position. [See maps, pp. 636 and 736.] On the northern or right bank of the Holston, a narrow table-land, or ridge, beginning about two miles east of the town, extends down the river to Lenoir's, some 24 miles. This ridge is generally elevated about 150 feet above the river, but with many higher points. Its width at Knoxville is about 1300 yards, and the valley bounding it on the north-west, parallel with the river, is perhaps 50 feet above that stream at the ordinary stage of water. The East Tennessee, Virginia and Georgia railroad is located along the valley, which was almost entirely clear of timber. At short intervals the ridge is cut through by small streams emptying into the Holston, two of which, called First and Second Creeks, run through the town at a distance apart of about one thousand yards. The main portion of Knoxville, as it existed at the time of the siege, occupied that portion of the table-land included between the two creeks, the river and the valley. East Knoxville was situated next east of First Creek, upon an elevation known as Temperance Hill. East of Temperance Hill, and separated from it by a depression in the ridge, is Mabry's Hill, the highest ground on the north side of the Holston within cannon-range of the town. Beyond this the ground, with a few minor elevations, gradually descends to the level of the valley. Flint Hill is immediately upon the bank of the river, south of Temperance Hill. Third Creek, a little more than a mile westward from Second Creek, forms the south-westerly limit of another natural division of the ridge, including the hill north-west from the college. North-westerly from the river are found successive ridges; the most important was occupied by the Confederates, across the valley a mile from our line. South of the Holston the ground rises in a series of prominent points, or knobs, the highest of which is directly opposite Knoxville on the prolongation of Gay street. These knobs form a range, the crest line of which is parallel with the river at an average distance from it of about half a mile, with a wide valley beyond.

On the Knoxville side of the Holston, our line rested upon the river about a quarter of a mile below the mouth of Second Creek, extended from there at an angle of about 82° with the river for 900 yards to Battery Noble,⚓ then, bending about 50° to the northward, continued a little more than 600 yards to Fort Sanders, where it changed direction about 65° to the eastward, and, overlooking the valley, followed the crest of the bluff, parallel with the general course of the river for some 1600 yards to Battery Wiltsie, opposite the railroad station, including, in this part of the line, Battery Zoellner, between Fort Sanders and Second Creek, Battery Galpin, just east of Second Creek, and Fort Comstock, between Battery Galpin and Battery Wiltsie. From the last named, with a slight change of direction toward the river, the line continued along the crest of the bluff, over Temperance Hill to Mabry's Hill, a distance of 2400 yards, including Battery Billingsley just west of First Creek, Fort Huntington Smith on Temperance Hill, Battery Clifton Lee and Battery Stearman in the depression between Temperance Hill and Mabry's Hill, and Fort Hill on the extreme easterly point of Mabry's Hill. From here it turned sharply to the southward for 1300 yards and reached the river at a ravine about 1000 yards above the mouth of First Creek. A continuous line of infantry cover connected all these positions, and dams were built at the crossing of First and Second Creeks which, by backing the water, formed considerable obstacles, especially in front of Temperance Hill, where the line was parallel with the course of First Creek for 1200 yards, and the pond impassable without bridges.

A short interior line was established from Fort Sanders to Second Creek, near its mouth. This included Fort Byington, built around the college. Another line extended from Temperance Hill to Flint Hill, terminating in Battery Fearns.

On the south side of the river such of the heights (four in number) as were necessary to the defense were occupied by detached works with extensions for infantry cover, insufficient, however, to make the line continuous, or even approximately so. Fort Stanley was built on the hill directly opposite Knoxville, and a line of ordinary rifle-trenches was carried eastward from it across the Sevierville road and to the adjacent height. The hill nearly opposite the mouth of Second Creek was occupied by Fort Dickerson, and the next one to the westward by Fort Higley.

The arrangements for the defense of the position on the north side of the Holston were necessarily made in the most hurried manner. The earth-works known as Fort Sanders and Fort Huntington Smith, intended for a very different condition of affairs, were so far advanced toward completion when Longstreet appeared before Knoxville, that their use without modification was compulsory. Neither of the plans was what it would have been had the works been designed for parts of a continuous line. Especially was this the case with respect to Fort Sanders, the trace of which was such that under the stress of circumstances its north-western bastion became a prominent salient of the main line, and notwithstanding the measures taken to remedy this objec-

⚓ The several positions along the line were not named until after the lines were established,—Fort Sanders on the 18th of November, and the others after the siege was raised. All were named after officers who had been killed during the siege or in the operations preceding it.—O. M. P.

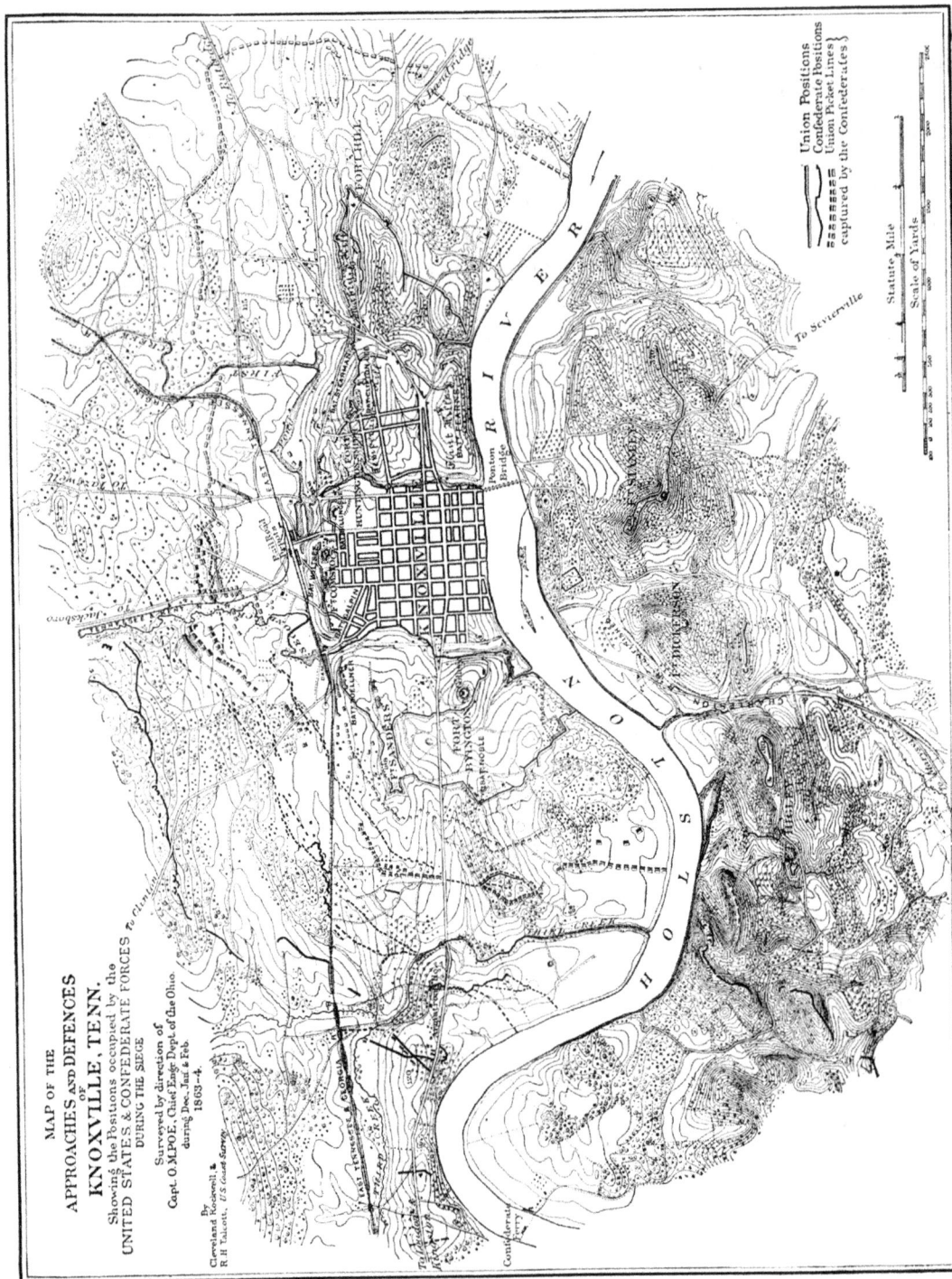

MAP OF THE
APPROACHES AND DEFENCES
OF
KNOXVILLE, TENN.
Showing the Positions occupied by the
UNITED STATES & CONFEDERATE FORCES
DURING THE SIEGE

Surveyed by direction of
Capt. O. M. POE, Chief Eng. Dept. of the Ohio
during Dec., Jan. & Feb.
1863-4.

By
Cleveland Rockwell &
R. H. Talcott, U.S. Coast Survey.

tionable feature, its existence caused us great anxiety. The sector without
fire of the bastion referred to (the one attacked) would have been a sector
without fire for the line, but for the arrangements made on either side of it to
overcome the defect as far as possible. The fire thus obtained in front of this
bastion was not all that could have been desired, but the event proved that
it was sufficient. That Longstreet's renowned infantry failed to carry it by
assault demonstrated that there were no very serious defects unprovided for.

As already stated, the head of Burnside's column appeared at Knoxville at daybreak on the 17th of November. It was met near Third Creek, and the organizations were directed to their respective stations, formed upon the lines, and told to dig, and to do it with all their might. By the middle of the forenoon all were hard at work. The locations of but few of the organizations were changed during the siege, and these but slightly.

Except the incomplete forts, Sanders and Huntington Smith, nothing in the way of defensive works had been previously contemplated. Lines of rifle-trenches soon appeared, only to grow rapidly into continuous infantry parapets. Batteries for the artillery were ready in the shortest possible time.

During the night of the 16th of November Sanders had crossed his division of cavalry to the north side of the river and moved out on the Loudon road to cover our forces, approaching from Campbell's Station, until they could get into position and make some progress in the construction of defensive works. Slowly falling back as the enemy advanced on the 17th, he finally made a stand with one brigade of about 700 men under his immediate command, upon a hill just north of the Loudon road, a mile from Fort Sanders and about 800 yards west from where that road crossed Third Creek; while the other brigade (two regiments of mounted infantry), commanded by Colonel C. D. Pennebaker, turned at bay where the Clinton road crossed the ridge about a mile north-west from Fort Sanders.

For the remainder of the 17th these commands stubbornly held their ground, in full view of our lines, the principal Confederate attacks being directed upon the position of Sanders, who kept up a fierce and gallant contest with Longstreet's infantry and Alexander's guns, ceasing only with the darkness. About 11 P. M. General Burnside sent for me, and upon reporting to him at his headquarters at Crozier's house, I found him in conversation with Sanders. He asked me how long it would take to make the works defensible, and was informed that it could be done by noon of the next day, the 18th. Turning to Sanders he asked him if he would maintain his position until that time, and received an assuring promise. Sanders accompanied me to my quarters, where we discussed the matter until after midnight, and then lay down upon the same blanket to get some rest, but before daylight he was called by the guard, and left to join his command.

As day dawned the attacks upon Sanders were renewed, with the evident determination to dislodge him in the shortest possible time. As hour after hour passed, and that cavalry continued to stand against the pressure, it excited the wonder of the rest of our army. The contest was very unequal, and occasionally a few of our men would leave their position behind the piles of fence rails which constituted their only cover, with the apparent intention of retreating. At such critical times Sanders would walk up to the rail piles and stand there erect, with fully half his height exposed to a terrific fire at short range, until every retreating man, as if ashamed of himself, would return to his proper place. He held his ground until noon as he had promised, and then, in accordance with an understanding with me, continued to hold it, intending to do so until actually driven away. At about half-past two he fell, mortally

THE NORTH-WESTERN BASTION OF FORT SANDERS, VIEWED FROM THE NORTH. FROM A WAR-TIME PHOTOGRAPH.

wounded, and the screen which he had so stubbornly interposed between the enemy and our hard-working troops was quickly rolled aside.

Every spadeful of earth turned while Sanders was fighting aided in making our position secure, and he had determined to sacrifice himself if necessary for the safety of the rest of the army. Hence he maintained his position so strenuously, and but for his fall it is possible he would have held it until night, as I sincerely believe he meant to do. His fine presence, soldierly bearing, extreme gallantry, and unvarying courtesy attached to him the incongruous elements composing his command, and enabled him to handle it as he did on this occasion, when its behavior was certainly worthy the commendation it received. The fort in front of which he fell was immediately named after him in commemoration of the service rendered.

Early on the 18th eight or ten of the enemy had established themselves in the upper story of the tower of a brick house which stood about 750 yards beyond Sanders's line, and from this advantageous position greatly annoyed his command by their accurate fire. He sent a request to Benjamin, in Fort Sanders, to try the effect upon these sharp-shooters of a few shots from his 20-pounder Parrotts. The distance was 2500 yards, but Benjamin's gunner put a shot directly through the compartment occupied by the sharp-shooters, badly wrecking it (as was ascertained by examination after the siege), and abating the nuisance. During the whole war I saw no prettier single shot.

By the night of the 18th our infantry trenches on the north side of the river had been made nearly continuous, and our heavier works were well advanced. The enemy's skirmishers pushed up in front of ours, and the siege was fairly on. On the 19th he extended to his left, and during the day threw shells into Knoxville from a battery posted on the Tazewell road, about a mile and a half from our main line. On the 20th the enemy's offensive lines began to appear, his right approaching the river near Armstrong's house just west of Third Creek. From there he extended toward the left across the valley and along the ridge beyond on a line nearly concentric with ours. The earth-works on each side seemed to grow like magic, but we were apparently doing more digging than they. Indeed, they never constructed any works of consequence east of the Jacksboro' road.

A large brick house, with two log barns, stood within the enemy's skirmish line in front of Fort Sanders, and served as cover for troublesome sharp-shooters. Why these buildings were not destroyed by us as we fell back I do not know, but it soon became evident that it must be done now, and the 17th Michigan Infantry was detailed for the purpose. At 9 P. M. the regiment, passing to the rear and left of Fort Sanders, advanced to our skirmish line, where they halted a few moments to adjust the line, and again moved forward. The enemy soon discovered the movement and opened fire, whereupon our men charged at a run, and quickly gained possession of the buildings; a baking-pan full of warm biscuits in the house indicating the completeness of the surprise. A party of five volunteers under charge of Major F. W. Swift had been formed to set fire to the buildings. These were effectually fired, and our men were half-way on their return to our lines before the light of the burning buildings revealed the party to the enemy, who then opened a cannonade upon them.

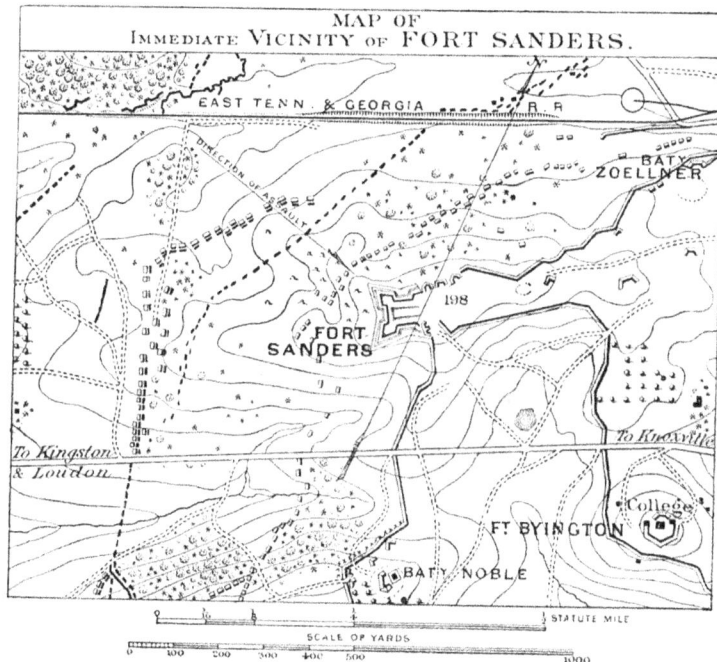

MAP OF IMMEDIATE VICINITY OF FORT SANDERS.

The siege and defensive operations progressed in the usual manner until the 22d, when we received information‡ that the enemy was constructing a raft at Boyd's Ferry, on the Holston, about six miles above Knoxville by the course of the river, intending to set it adrift in the hope that it would reach our pontoon-bridge and carry it away, thus breaking our communication with the south side. About dark we began stretching an iron cable boom across the river above the bridge, with a view to catching the raft. The cable was about a thousand feet long, formed by linking together all the iron bars we could get, and was borne by wooden floats. Under my personal supervision the boom was completed by 9 o'clock next morning.

On the evening of the 23d the enemy advanced upon our skirmishers in front of Fort Comstock and drove them back, but not until they had set fire to all the buildings in the immediate vicinity. We regained the position next

‡ John C. Phillips, of Chicago, captain and chief of artillery during the siege, writes to the editors that this information came in the form of a mes- sage in a bottle sent down the river by a Union woman living near the point where the raft was being constructed.

morning. Nearly due west from Fort Sanders the enemy had advanced his line to within about 600 yards of the fort, and had thrown up a continuous line of infantry trench, with its right resting on the railroad and extending about 300 yards to the left. Early in the morning of the 24th a detail of 169 men of the 2d Michigan Infantry attacked and carried this work. After they had held it for some time without reënforcements, the enemy made a counter-attack in largely increased force, with lamentable results to us, our men being driven back with a loss of nearly half their number.

Strange as it may seem, this sortie was made without my knowledge, and although I made considerable effort afterward to ascertain who was responsible for it, I never succeeded. It would be difficult to conceive a more ill-advised movement. It would have been proper if we had intended to bring on a general engagement, in which case the sortie should have been supported with our whole force. If such was not the intention, the sortie should not have been made at all. Carried out in the manner it was, the affair was simply murderous. This is strong language, but every word of it is justified by the unneces-

BRIGADIER-GENERAL WILLIAM P. SANDERS, KILLED AT KNOXVILLE. FROM A PHOTOGRAPH.

sary loss of about eighty-three of our very best men. The notes which I made at the time show that if I could have found any one to stand sponsor for the order, my condemnation of it would have then been quite as decided as now.

About the same time the enemy crossed the Holston below his lines and unsuccessfully attacked our forces on the south side of the river. He established batteries of rifled guns on the heights nearly opposite the mouth of Third Creek (never occupied by us), distant about 2300 yards from Fort Sanders, rendering it necessary to defilade this work against them.

The reports of a destructive raft being renewed, another boom, 1500 feet long, and made of long timbers fastened together at the ends by fifth chains from the wagon trains, was stretched across the river above the first one.

Prior to our occupation of Knoxville, the enemy had begun the erection of an earth-work, called by them Fort Loudon, on the site afterward occupied by Fort Sanders. A second growth of pines, averaging about five inches in diameter, thickly covered the hillside in front, and were cut down by them, leaving stumps perhaps eighteen inches high. The necessity for using every possible means of obstructing the approach over the sector without fire in front of the north-western bastion of Fort Sanders, included in the area covered by these stumps, was evident to every one, and became more pressing as the probability of an assault at this point grew more apparent. At this time Mr. Hoxie, in charge of the railroad property at Knoxville, informed me that he had a lot of old telegraph wire at the depot which he thought might be of service to us as an obstruction. Its use as a net-work entanglement, by carrying it from stump to stump over the sector without fire referred to, was so obvious that no time was lost in putting it in place. The part it played in causing the repulse was much overrated. Owing to its rusty color, nearly that of the pine litter just under it, and the imperfect light of the foggy morning, it doubtless did have some effect in breaking up the coherency of the assaulting column, and may possibly have detained it long enough to permit the defense to deliver a couple of rounds more, a matter of some consequence.

The wet, foggy, and generally disagreeable weather of the preceding days still continued, when, at about 11 o'clock on the night of the 28th, our picket lines in front of Fort Sanders were attacked with such spirit as to indicate an important movement, and after sharp skirmishing for some length of time were finally carried. This was, in fact, the prelude to an assault upon the main work, and had for its immediate effect to put us on the alert and keep us in readiness for the serious business which we knew was close at hand.

The enemy's arrangements for the assault provided that it be made in two columns, from McLaws's division, directed against the north-west angle of Fort Sanders, the one on the left to be composed of Wofford's brigade, in column of regiments, with the 16th Georgia leading; while the other, formed in like order, was to consist of Humphreys's brigade, led by the 13th Mississippi, and closely followed by three regiments of Bryan's brigade. The attack was to be made with fixed bayonets, without cheering or firing a shot, and the men were to be urged to rush forward with a determination to succeed. The sharp-shooters were to keep up a continuous fire into the embrasures of the fort and along the adjacent works, to prevent the use of artillery against the assaulting force and to disturb the fire of all arms. Anderson's brigade, following the main attack, was to carry the works about a hundred yards to the left, and, in case the assault on Fort Sanders should prove successful, was then to wheel to the left, and, followed by Benning's and Jenkins's brigades, sweep down our lines to the eastward. But if the main attack should fail, Anderson was to wheel to the right and endeavor to carry Fort Sanders from the rear. Kershaw's brigade was to advance to the assault of the works on the right of the fort as soon as it had fallen. The unassigned brigades of McLaws's and Jenkins's divisions, together with the brigades of Bushrod Johnson and Gracie, were to be held in readiness to follow up any success. Thus the plan of assault had been well studied, carefully elaborated, and clearly formulated. The preparations for resisting it were the wire entanglements already described, a slight abatis, the strong profile of Fort Sanders, and the arrangements for both a direct and a cross fire in front of the salient not only from the garrison of the fort itself, but also from the troops occupying the adjacent intrenchments.

THE NORTH-WESTERN BASTION OF FORT SANDERS,
VIEWED FROM THE SOUTH-WESTERN BASTION.
FROM A PHOTOGRAPH.

Fort Sanders was laid out in strict accordance with the rules for constructing bastioned earth-works, but upon shorter exterior lines than were desirable. It was built upon an irregular quadrilateral of which the western side was 95 yards, the northern 125 yards, the eastern 85 yards, and the southern 125 yards; the north-western bastion being traced in the right angle between the first two sides. The western front was completed, and the two adjoining ones had been carried far enough to give us the advantage of their flanking arrangements. The eastern front had been intentionally left open. Provision had been made by pan-coupés for an artillery fire along the capitals of the two completed bastions, and a 12-pounder gun had been placed in the one attacked. The trace of the interior crest was so located on the slopes of the hill that when a parade of about forty feet in width had been formed, the undisturbed ground behind it served some of the minor purposes of a traverse. The ditch was made twelve feet wide at the bastion faces, and from six to eight feet in depth, depending upon the accidents of the ground, the average being about seven feet. The result of this location of the interior crest and depth of ditch, was an unusually high relief to the work, especially at the north-western bastion. The scarps were practically vertical, and the berme at the foot of the exterior slope was cut away. The counterscarps were continued until they intersected, and all the material between them and the curtain excavated to the general level of the bottom of the ditch, thus obviating all dead angles. A banquette was formed in the counterscarp at the north-western salient, of sufficient extent for the location of about forty men, whose fire could be delivered in the direction of the capital. In addition to the ordinary flank fire, three 12-pounders were so located in notches in the immediate eastward extension of the northern front as to admit of their firing into the left flank of the assaulting column; and a fire, more or less efficient, could be delivered over the same ground from our intrenchments as far eastward as Battery Zoellner. A similar fire into their front and right flank was obtained from our lines to the southward of Fort Sanders as far as Battery Noble.

The garrison of Fort Sanders at the time of the assault, usually estimated at about 500 men, consisted of Benjamin's and Buckley's batteries and one section of Roemer's (four 20-pounder Parrotts, six 12-pounder Napoleons, and two 3-inch rifled guns), and an infantry force made up of some 120 men of the 79th New York, 75 men of the 29th Massachusetts, 60 men of the 2d Michigan, and 80 men of the 20th Michigan. About forty men of the 2d Michigan, under command of Captain Charles H. Hodskin, occupied the banquette in the counterscarp salient as long as the position was tenable, and then ran through the ditch to the southward; they entered the fort around the south-eastern angle as they had been instructed to do, and took further part in the defense.

The number actually within the fort at the moment of the supreme struggle and repulse probably did not exceed 440 men. The discrepancy arises from the different ways of reckoning the limits of the fort, due to the open eastern front. The smaller estimate includes only the troops that were within the bastioned trace. Yet some very effective work was done against the assaulting column by the fire coming from the intrenchments beyond the original Fort Sanders, and it has always seemed to me only fair that troops delivering this fire should be counted in estimating the strength of the garrison, in which case the total would be increased to more than three times the number given.

About 6 A. M. on Sunday, November 29th, the enemy opened a heavy artillery fire upon Fort Sanders, to which no reply was made, because our limited supply of ammunition made it necessary to reserve it for use at a more critical moment. The fire continued for about twenty minutes and then slackened, whereupon the columns moved to the assault, and were at once met by all the fire that could be concentrated upon them from our lines. Encountering the wire entanglements, their organization was somewhat disturbed, but the movement was not seriously checked thereby, nor did the slight abatis retard it. Although suffering from the terribly destructive fire to which they were subjected, they soon reached the outer brink of the ditch. There could be no pause at that point, and, leaping into the ditch in such numbers as nearly to fill it, they endeavored to scale the walls. Having no scaling-ladders, a portion of the men, scrambling over the shoulders of their comrades, planted the battle-flags of the 13th and 17th Mississippi and the 16th Georgia upon the parapet, but every man who rallied to them was either killed or captured, and the flags were taken.

Meanwhile those who remained in the ditch found themselves under a deadly flank fire of musketry and canister, supplemented by shells thrown as hand-grenades from inside the fort, without the slightest possibility of returning a blow. Advance and retreat were about equally difficult, and it needed but a very short exposure to convince them that if any were to leave the ditch alive it could only be by the promptest surrender. Those who were able to walk were brought through the ditch to the south-eastern angle and there entered our lines as prisoners. Such of the assaulting forces as had not entered the ditch fell back, at first sullenly and slowly, but flesh and blood could not stand the storm of shot and shell that was poured upon them, and they soon broke in confused retreat.

The assault had been gallantly made, but was repulsed in little more time than is required to describe it. When the result became apparent Longstreet directed the withdrawal of the supporting brigade, but the order did not reach Anderson in time to prevent his troops from pushing on as though the assault had been successful. They swerved, however, somewhat to their left, and attacked a short distance to the eastward of the designated point, only to meet with as decided, though not so bloody, a repulse.

The assaulting columns were rallied under partial cover some five or six hundred yards from Fort Sanders and there reorganized, but no further open attempt to carry our lines was made.

Many reasons have been assigned for the failure of this assault, and there is some difference of opinion in regard to the matter. Some of those opposed to us, of unquestioned ability and fairness, have attributed it to the warning given us by taking our picket line the night before, the insufficient use of their artillery, and the improper direction taken by two of the columns, resulting in their intermingling and consequent confusion. The opinion has been confidently expressed that a subsequent assault would have been successful. All this assumes, first, that we were not already vigilant and waiting for the attack; second, that a heavy and continued artillery fire would have greatly damaged and demoralized us; third, that the confusion arising from the convergence of the advancing columns would not have occurred again; fourth, that the works were " very faulty in plan and very easy to take by a properly managed assault"; and last, but not least, that the troops of the enemy were better than ours. The first of these assumptions is erroneous; the second greatly exaggerated; the

BRIGADIER-GENERAL E. P. ALEXANDER, C. S. A.
FROM A PHOTOGRAPH.

third might have been verified, but again might not; the fourth is correct only within the limits and to the extent already explained; and the last has no evidence to sustain it.

No one is more ready and willing than the writer to admit the excellence of the troops that fought us at Knoxville. They had few equals, and I believe no superiors. But in making this admission I do not abate one particle of my confidence in the valor and persistency of those who opposed them. They possessed those qualities in as high degree as General Longstreet's men or any others, and the succession of events had only served to improve their morale. It may fairly be doubted whether any disaster to our arms was imminent.

Again, the repulse may have been due to the existence of fewer faults in the works than supposed; to the measures adopted by us to remedy the faults which did exist; ♭ to the passive obstacles of wire entanglements, depth of ditch and unusual relief of the parapet; to the enemy's error in deciding it to be unnecessary to provide scaling-ladders for the storming party; and, finally and emphatically, to a sufficient garrison of the coolest, bravest, and most determined men. Each of these reasons seems to me to have contributed its share to the result, and some of them were surely of much graver moment than any of those assigned by the other side.

The successful resistance of the 29th did not lead to any remission of labor on our defenses. Work was continued by the troops with the energy that had characterized their efforts thus far, but the enemy gave little indication of a purpose to do anything further upon their works of attack. On the 1st of December large trains belonging to the enemy were seen moving to the eastward, and again on the 3d and 4th and on the night of the 4th his troops were withdrawn and the siege was raised. We had not yet heard the result of General Grant's operations at Chattanooga.

The signal defeat of Bragg at Missionary Ridge and the happy conclusion of the siege of Knoxville confirmed our hold upon the direct line of communication between the enemy's forces east and west and achieved the permanent relief of the friends of our cause in east Tennessee.

The conduct of the men who stood in the trenches at Knoxville cannot be overpraised. Half starved, with clothing tattered and torn, they endured without a murmur every form of hardship and exposure that falls to the lot of the soldier. The question with them was not whether they could withstand the assaults of the enemy, but simply whether sufficient food could be obtained to enable them to keep their places in the line. That they were not reduced to the last extremity in this regard is due to the supplies sent in by the loyalists of the French Broad settlements, who took advantage of Longstreet's inability to invest the place completely, and under cover of the night-fogs floated down to us such food and forage as they could collect.

♭ "On the morning of December 6th I rode from Marysville into Knoxville, and met General Burnside. . . . We examined his lines of fortifications, which were a wonderful production for the short time allowed in their selection of ground and construction of work. It seemed to me that they were nearly impregnable. We examined the redoubt named 'Sanders,' where on the Sunday previous three brigades of the enemy had assaulted and met a bloody repulse."— Extract from General Sherman's official report of December 19th, 1863.

LONGSTREET AT KNOXVILLE.

BY E. PORTER ALEXANDER, BRIGADIER-GENERAL, C. S. A.

AFTER the return of the Army of Northern Virginia from Gettysburg, it took position south of the Rapidan River, in the vicinity of Orange Court House, to recuperate from the losses and fatigue of the campaign. We settled ourselves in comfortable camps among the wooded hills, enjoyed better rations than we ever got again, gradually collected horses, recruits, conscripts, and returning sick and wounded, and altogether we felt about as well satisfied with the situation and prospect as we had ever done before. The enjoyment of our pleasant camps and still pleas-

anter rest was suddenly broken, on September 9th, by orders for Hood's and McLaws's divisions of Longstreet's corps, about 11,000 strong, with my battalion of artillery, 23 guns, to go under the personal command of General Longstreet to reenforce Bragg in Georgia.

It was clear that our now, however, adversary, the Army of the Potomac, could not resume the offensive for some months, and there would be ample time to send this force out to enable Bragg to crush Rosecrans, and bring it back to Virginia before it would be needed there. It was the only occasion during the war, I believe, when the Confederates availed themselves of the possession of the interior and shorter lines, and transferred a force of any magnitude rapidly from the eastern to the western army to meet an emergency, and then to return.

The orders were received September 9th, and the troops were put in motion immediately for Petersburg, whence we were to have railroad transportation to the vicinity of Chattanooga via Wilmington, N. C., and Augusta and Atlanta, Ga. This line at the time was the only one open from Virginia to Georgia, the East Tennessee line, the only other then existing, being held by the enemy at Knoxville. Consequently it was taxed with the entire business of the Confederacy between those States, and that it managed to do it at all has always seemed to me a feat in railroad management deserving great praise. The roads had had but a small business before the war, and their equipment and motive power were light even for those days. The gauges were not uniform, and often the tracks of connecting roads were joined through the cities only by lines of drays, and there was no interchange of cars. There was no manufactory of locomotives in the South, and but one small rolling-mill, at Atlanta, that could make a rail. Yet, in spite of all these drawbacks and the enormous business suddenly thrown upon them, and frequent raids by the enemy, destroying bridges, tearing up tracks, burning ties, and bending and twisting rails, the railroads always came up again smiling, and stuck to the contest as faithfully as did the army.

My battalion brought up the rear, leaving Petersburg September 17th, and arriving at Ringgold, the railroad terminus near Chickamauga, on the 25th. Our artillery was distributed about our lines, the station of my own battalion being on Lookout Mountain, whence we threw shells over the enemy's territory, and fought daily with a vicious little battery in Moccasin Bend, almost directly under us. This battery had nearly buried itself in the ground under high parapets, and fired up at us like a man shooting at a squirrel in a tree. We propped our trails high up in the air to depress the muzzles, and tried to mash our opponents into the earth with solid shot and percussion-shells: but we never hurt them much, and when we left the mountain they were still as lively as ever.

It was at last decided by General Bragg not to attempt to manœuvre Rosecrans out of Chattanooga, but to detach Longstreet and send him up to try to capture Burnside, who was at Knoxville with a force of about 12,000 effective men. On the night of November 4th we withdrew from Lookout Mountain, and the next day marched to Tyner's Station, whence, with Longstreet's two divisions of infantry, Hood's (under Jenkins) and McLaws's, about 10,000 infantry,‡ we were to be taken by rail as far as Sweetwater. The infantry

were sent in advance, and the railroad was so taxed to do this that we were detained at Tyner's until the 10th, and meanwhile nearly starved, as rations had been provided for only half that time.

At length, about noon on the 10th, a train of flat cars came for us and the guns and men were loaded, the horses being sent afoot. It was a cold and windy night, and we suffered a great deal on the open cars. There was a very insufficient water and wood supply on the road, and the troops had to bail water and chop up fence rails for the engine. The journey of only sixty miles occupied the whole afternoon and night. On the 13th we moved from Sweetwater with the infantry and a pontoon-train, and our artillery was reënforced by Leyden's battalion of 12 guns, giving us in all 35. Owing to the scarcity of horses we were compelled to use oxen to haul the caissons.

We encamped near Sweetwater for two days, while secret reconnoissances were made of the enemy's position across the Tennessee River at Loudon, and commissary, quartermaster, and ordnance trains were organized and equipped. On the 13th, Friday, we marched to Huff's Ferry, about two miles by land below Loudon, which point had been selected for our crossing. Everything was kept out of sight of the enemy, and soon after dark some pontoons were carried by hand to the river, a half mile below the ferry, and a party of infantry ferried over, to try to surround and capture the Federal picket which was posted on their side. This part of the programme, however, failed, from the vigilance of the Federal sentries. They all escaped, and probably carried the news to Burnside that we were crossing in force, for early next morning a strong reconnoissance was pushed on us by the enemy as the last of our troops were crossing the pontoon which had been constructed during the night. We drove it back, and organizing a strong advance-guard under Lieutenant-Colonel (afterward General) T. M. Logan, of Hampton's Legion, with Parker's battery of my battalion, we pushed forward vigorously in the effort to bring Burnside to bay and defeat him before he could get back and concentrate behind the fortifications about Knoxville. This he had set out to do as soon as he appreciated the situation, sending his trains ahead and covering them with his whole force. For three days there ensued a sort of running skirmish covering the whole distance to Knoxville, about thirty miles. It was not rapid progress, but the days were short, the roads axle-deep in mud, and a strong rear-guard of the enemy skirmished with us for every hill and wood and stream on the road. Twice — at Lenoir's the first afternoon, the 15th, and at Campbell's Station the next — we seemed to have brought him to bay, and behind our advance-guard our whole force was brought up and formed for attack. But the approach of night prevented an action on both occa-

‡ On p. 709 General Grant speaks of Bragg's grave mistakes in the Chattanooga campaign, "first, in sending away his ablest corps commander, with over 20,000 troops; second, in sending away a division of troops on the eve of battle." The force originally sent with Longstreet included, besides Hood and McLaws, 5000

of Wheeler's cavalry, and these commands were all engaged in the Knoxville campaign. On the 22d of November, two brigades of Buckner's division (Gracie's and Bushrod Johnson's) were sent from Chattanooga and reached Knoxville by the 28th, but were not actively engaged.— EDITORS.

THE NORTH-WESTERN BASTION OF FORT SANDERS, SHOWING THE GROUND OVER WHICH THE
CONFEDERATES CHARGED. FROM A PHOTOGRAPH.

sions, though on the latter we got in a sharp and pretty artillery duel over some nice open ground unusually favorable for it, during which one of our guns, a 20-pounder Parrott, exploded, but fortunately without killing any one. Here we found out that we had opposite to us an old friend, Benjamin's battery of 20-pounder Parrotts, which had been our vis-à-vis at Fredericksburg, where it had pounded us from "Mary Scott's Hill."

The night of the third day, the 17th, Burnside was safe in Knoxville, and we encamped at Hazen's, a short distance off. The next day we began reconnoitering for the best place to assault.

A Federal cavalry brigade, under General W. P. Sanders, held a line of rail breastworks on a hill near the Armstrong house, and interfered seriously with our freedom of motion. Our skirmishers having vainly tried to move them, and artillery ammunition being too scarce for much of a cannonade on a minor point, we got up two of Taylor's Napoleons, so they could not be seen, behind a house which stood about 250 yards from the enemy's line, and asked for two regiments of infantry to charge it as soon as we made an impression. All being ready, the guns were run out from behind the house and opened vigorously with solid shot, being helped also by Moody's 24-pounder howitzers with shrapnel, a short distance to the left. At the close range Taylor made the rails fly at every shot, and the enemy began to desert them

rapidly and run back over the hill. Then the 2d and 3d South Carolina regiments of Kershaw's brigade rose from their cover and dashed at them. Sanders and his officers rallied their men gallantly and brought most of them back to the line, and poured a heavy fire upon the Carolinians. The latter advanced rapidly without returning it until they reached two cedar-trees within thirty yards of the enemy, when they halted, lay down, and opened fire. This was from a misapprehension of their orders, which were not to go farther forward than the enemy's line near the cedar-trees. In three minutes, however, the mistake was appreciated, and, rising with a yell, they dashed upon and carried the rail breastwork, killing and capturing quite a number of the enemy. ⚓

On the 19th, the enemy being now pretty closely confined to the town, we began preparations to assault him. It was first necessary to study his lines and find the most favorable point.

The town had been partly fortified a year before by the Confederates, and the topography being generally favorable to defense, it was not easy to find a weak spot, especially as we were all unfamiliar with the locality, and without even maps of the city.

It soon appeared that there was but one point of the lines which it was possible to assault with any hope of success. That was a fort which had been started by the Confederates under the name

⚓ This action was very sharp for a small affair and was well fought on both sides. When our infantry line halted and lay down, Captain S. Winthrop, of my staff, galloped up to and through them as they rose, and right up to the breastworks. A dozen muskets could be seen blazing at him, and he fell forward on his horse's neck with a bullet through the collar-bone. He had been a captain in Her Majesty's 24th regiment, and came to the Confederacy to get a taste of active service, and on other

occasions than this also fully sustained the reputation of British pluck.

The Federal general, Sanders, was mortally wounded in this skirmish. He was from Mississippi, and I believe was a distant relative of President Davis. We had been intimate at West Point, and had met in San Francisco in 1861, as I was about resigning to cast my fortunes with my native State. We parted with no anticipations of such a meeting.— E. P. A.

of Fort Loudon, and had been finished by the Federals and by them called Fort Sanders. It was upon a hill that fell off to the north-west, so that a large force could be marched under cover and approach within two hundred yards of the fort without being exposed to view or to fire either from the fort or the adjacent lines on either side, which here made an obtuse angle. [See p. 739.]

All of our artillery, thirty-four guns, was posted in the most available positions to fire upon this fort and enfilade the adjacent lines, except four howitzers, which were rigged as mortars to drop shells behind the parapets and to search out spaces sheltered from direct fire. To accomplish this, skids were prepared inclined at an angle of forty-five degrees, one end resting on the ground and the other on a horizontal pole supported about six feet from the ground by forked posts. The axle of the howitzer was run up on these skids, raising the wheels in the air on each side of the skids, and leaving the trail on the ground between them, until the piece had an elevation of about sixty degrees. I had experimented with the arrangement in Virginia, and also at Chattanooga, and found it to work nicely and to give very fair mortar practice. Of course the range was regulated by the charge of powder used. We also rigged up an old flat-boat and made a ferry with some telegraph wire, by which we carried Parker's rifle-guns to the south side of the river and established a battery on a commanding hill, from which we could enfilade the western front of the fort at a range of 2600 yards. All of our guns were protected by earth-works.

These arrangements occupied us closely until Tuesday, the 24th. The attack was ordered to begin at sunrise on the 25th, and was to be made as follows: First, the mortars were to open and get the range by slow and deliberate practice. Next, the direct-fire guns were to do the same. Next, a strong line of sharp-shooters was to capture and occupy the enemy's line of rifle-pits in which their pickets were posted, and from these pits, an average distance of 200 yards, maintain a concentrated fire upon the parapet and embrasures of the fort. Next, all thirty of the guns and mortars were to pour a rapid fire into the fort for about a half hour, to dismount its guns and demoralize its garrison, and under cover of this fire and the sharp-shooters the storming column, previously massed under shelter, was to advance. As it approached, the guns would shift their fire to the right and left, and the mortars would resume their natural functions as howitzers and limber up and follow the storming column.

On the night of the 24th we learned that Bushrod Johnson's and Gracie's brigades, about 2600 men, were on their way to reënforce us, and would arrive the next night. The attack was accordingly postponed to await their arrival. With them came General Leadbetter, chief engineer to Bragg, who had been stationed at Knoxville and was familiar with its fortifications. Under his advice Longstreet again postponed the attack, and the next day went in person with him to look at the enemy's lines above the town, with a view to making the attack there. On their return Thursday night I was ordered to withdraw our guns from the south side of the river, as it was intended to move up above the town and make the assault on Mabry's Hill.

On Friday I accompanied Generals Longstreet, Leadbetter, and others on a careful reconnoissance of this locality with a force of cavalry under General Wheeler, who drove in the enemy's pickets. This reconnoissance convinced every one that an attack in that quarter was impossible. The hill was strongly fortified, the approaches inundated, and there was no cover within a mile for the formation and advance of an assaulting column. It was unanimously decided to go back to the plan of assaulting Fort Sanders, and I was ordered to get the guns back upon the hills across the river early Saturday morning. This was done, but the day turned out rainy and the assault was again postponed until Sunday, the 28th. So General Leadbetter's advent cost us three as valuable days as the sun ever shone upon. Meanwhile a rumor reached us that Bragg had had a severe battle at Chattanooga, and had been defeated and driven back to Dalton.

Late on Saturday afternoon General Longstreet suddenly changed the plan of attack (I believe under advice of General Leadbetter) and ordered that instead of beginning at sunrise, and being preceded by a crushing fire of artillery concentrated on the fort and covered by an enveloping swarm of sharp-shooters, a surprise should be attempted just before dawn by the infantry alone. This was a bitter disappointment to the artillery, after so many days spent in preparation. We believe that in daylight, with our aid, the result would have been different.

About 11 o'clock that night our infantry skirmishers were ordered to move forward and capture the enemy's pickets, which was successfully accomplished with a little firing, and our sharp-shooters established themselves in the enemy's line of rifle-pits within 150 yards of the fort. But it put the enemy on the alert, and during the rest of the night they fired occasional rounds of canister over our ground. The troops were brought up as soon as the rifle-pits were taken and formed in the sheltered ground in the rear. Those assigned to the storming of the fort were Humphreys's Mississippi brigade, and Bryan's and Wofford's Georgia brigades (the latter under Colonel Ruff), all of McLaws's division. Anderson's Georgia brigade, of Jenkins's division, was to support their left flank. The brigades averaged about one thousand men each.

The night was wretched, the temperature freezing, and a fine mist falling. The troops lay upon their arms without fires and suffered greatly.

At the earliest indication of dawn three signal-guns were fired in rapid succession from different batteries. Their shells were visible like meteors in the air and they exploded over the fort. Instantly the recumbent ranks of gray sprang to their feet and formed for a charge, not so famous in history as Pickett's charge at Gettysburg, and not so inspiriting a sight to see, for only the flashes of guns were visible in the dim light, but a charge that illustrated as well as Pickett's or any other ever made those splendid qualities of Longstreet's infantry which made them at once an admiration and a delight to their comrades in the artillery.

For a few minutes about a dozen guns poured a hot fire into the angle of the lines back of the fort, and the success with which they threw their shells about it, even in the dim light, made it all the harder to bear that the plan of attack had been changed and the artillery was not allowed to try its full strength. Then we ceased firing to leave a clear field for the storming column, except a few shots from a battery that could reach the ground in rear of the fort.

Meanwhile the assaulting column formed, advanced to the line of rifle-pits, and then swarmed over them and rushed for the fort. Almost immediately they found themselves in an entanglement of telegraph wires stretched a few inches above the ground and fastened to stumps and stakes. This, however, was quickly broken up, and the men pressed forward rapidly to the ditch around the fort, receiving a severe musketry fire from its parapet and two or three discharges of canister from guns which were able to reach a part of the ground traversed. It was impossible, however, to maintain ranks in this rapid advance, in darkness, over unknown ground with such obstacles, and under so close a fire. It resulted that the three brigades converged in a mass and without order around the north-west bastion. It was here that the ditch was supposed to be easily passable.

On the western face, indeed, it proved to be only about four-and-a-half feet deep, and ordinarily a ditch of that depth would not be a serious obstacle. But that morning the ground was frozen and very slippery, and, in addition, Colonel O. M. Poe, General Burnside's chief engineer, anticipating an assault, had made a very important variation in the ordinary profile of the ditch and parapet. Ordinarily there is left a space of about a foot between the edge of the ditch and the foot of the parapet, which space is called the " berme." [See cut, p. 750.]

It will be readily seen that to a man attempting to scale the parapet the berme is a great assistance, giving a foothold whence it is easy to rush up the exterior slope, which cannot be made steeper than forty-five degrees. Here the berme had been entirely cut away. To the right and left of the western face of the bastion the ditch grew deeper until it reached ten feet in places, and the parapet was raised in places by cotton bales. The advance was, of course, checked by the ditch, and the men generally swarmed along the edge, uncertain what

to do, and firing into the embrasures and at such of the enemy as ventured to show their heads over the parapet. This soon silenced the direct fire upon them from the parapet, except an occasional musket raised overhead to the level of the interior crest and fired without aim. The fort was so nearly silenced that looking on from the guns we thought it had surrendered, though some fire continued to come from the left.

Meanwhile many of the officers, color-bearers, and men jumped into the ditch and attempted to scale the parapet. The slippery slopes and the absence of a berme prevented their success in such numbers as to accomplish any result, and the gallant fellows going up one by one were shot down

FORT STANLEY, KNOXVILLE. FROM A PHOTOGRAPH.

from the inside as fast as they crowned the parapet. Nowhere in the war was individual example more splendidly illustrated than on that fatal slope and in that bloody ditch.

Some of the battle-flags were planted on the exterior crest and maintained there for some time by a succession of color-bearers. ↓ For fully twenty minutes the men stood around the ditch unable to get at their adversaries, but unwilling to retreat. Lieutenant Benjamin, commanding the artillery within the fort, made hand-grenades of his shells and exploded several within the ditch. Longstreet, seeing the flash of their explosions, and thinking them to be our own shells falling short, ordered the cessation of the slight artillery fire which we had continued to throw on the flanks and beyond the fort. [See note, p. 744.] At last, daylight having succeeded dawn, and further effort being plainly hopeless, the men sulkily withdrew. As the main force fell back Anderson's brigade of Jenkins's division, which was to take up the

---

↓ Colonel S. Z. Ruff, 18th Georgia, commanding Wofford's brigade; Colonel H. P. Thomas, of the 16th Georgia; and Colonel Kennon McElroy, 13th Mississippi, were killed, and Lieutenant-Colonel Fiser, 17th Mississippi, lost an arm upon the parapet. Adjutant T. W. Cumming, of the 16th Georgia, penetrated the

fort through an embrasure and was captured inside, assuring his captors that they would all be his prisoners within a few minutes. Lieutenant Munger, of the 9th Georgia, got into another embrasure, and, finding himself alone, emptied a revolver at the gunners and made his escape.— E. P. A.

attack upon the left of the assaulting column only in case of its success, unwilling to see the assault fail without trying it themselves, rushed forward to the ditch. Longstreet endeavored to have them stopped, but was too late. They repeated the scenes of the first attack, and after losing nearly two hundred men they likewise withdrew. The ranks were re-formed, however, close behind the line of the

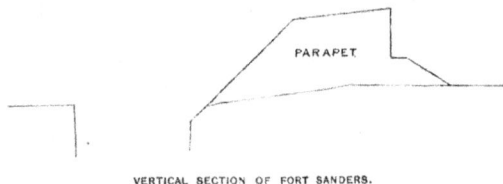

PARAPET

VERTICAL SECTION OF FORT SANDERS.

enemy's rifle-pits, which our sharp-shooters still occupied. It had been a bloody repulse, though occupying but about forty minutes. ⌡

Soon after the repulse I heard, with great delight, that Jenkins had asked and obtained permission to make a fresh attempt, for I felt the utmost confidence that a concentrated fire by daylight from our 34 guns and mortars, with 1000 sharp-shooters whom we could shelter within close range, could silence the fort entirely, enabling a storming column to plant ladders, fill the ditch with fascines, and cut footholds in the scarp, so that an overwhelming force might reach the interior. But before arrangements could be made Longstreet received official intelligence of Bragg's disaster and an order to abandon the siege of Knoxville and to move promptly to join Bragg. A renewal of the attack was, therefore, thought inexpedient, and orders were at once given to move all trains to the rear, in preparation for a retreat southward that night.

Under cover of night it was intended that we should abandon the siege and get a good start on our march to join Bragg, but before nightfall we got news from Bragg himself that a large force under Sherman was being moved to intercept us, and that an early junction with him was impossible. Under these circumstances it was finally decided to remain and threaten Knoxville as long as possible, and draw Sherman off from the pursuit of Bragg, and then to retreat northward into east Tennessee. We remained before Knoxville until the night of December 4th.

About noon the next day we encamped at Blain's Cross-roads, having made eighteen miles; that was, I think, about the very worst night march I ever went through. The roads were in fearful

condition, and in the inky darkness and pouring rain neither men nor animals could see. Frequently guns or wagons would be mired so that the column behind would be blocked in the mud until extra teams and men at the wheels could set the column going for a few minutes. Strict orders had been given that the men should not use fence rails for fuel, but that night they were ignored, and miles of fence were fired merely to light up the road.

I recall some incidents illustrating how poorly our army was provided with even prime necessaries, although we were in our own country. We were so badly off for horse-shoes that on the advance to Knoxville we stripped the shoes from all the dead horses, and we killed for the purpose all the wounded and broken-down animals, both our own and those left behind by the enemy. During the siege the river brought down to us a number of dead horses and mules, thrown in within the town. We watched for them, took them out, and got the shoes and nails from their feet. Our men were nearly as badly off as the animals — perhaps worse, as they did not have hoofs. I have myself seen bloody stains on frozen ground, left by the barefooted where our infantry had passed. We of the artillery took the shoes off the drivers and gave them to the cannoneers who had to march.

Early in the advance Longstreet gave permission to the men to "swap" shoes with the prisoners whenever any were taken, but each man was strictly required to have something to "swap," and not leave the prisoner barefoot. It was quite an amusing sight (to us) to see a ragged rebel with his feet tied up in a sort of raw beef-hide moccasin, which the men learned to make, come up to a squad of prisoners, inspect their feet, and select the one he would "swap" with. Generally, however, the prisoners took it all very good-humoredly, guyed one another, and swapped jokes also with the swappers. It looked a little rough, but, as one of the victims said, "When a man is captured, his shoes are captured too."

On Sunday the 6th we marched fifteen miles farther, to Rutledge; on the 8th seventeen more, to Mooresburg; and on the 9th nine more, in the direction of Rogersville. Here we remained until the 14th, when we marched back, hoping to be able to surprise and capture a small force of the enemy that had followed us to Bean's Station and had become separated from its support. ⌐

We spent the winter between Russellville and Greenville, living off the country, having occasional

⌡ Our losses had been 129 killed, 458 wounded, and 226 captured,—total, 813. The enemy's loss inside the fort was, I believe, only about 20.— E. P. A.

⌐ Gracie's brigade had quite a sharp engagement here, General Gracie being severely wounded, and Kershaw's and Bushrod Johnson's brigades and two of my batteries were slightly engaged; but darkness came on before we could get a sufficient force into position and line, and under cover of it the enemy retreated. It had been intended to cut off his retreat with a force of cavalry, but the plan miscarried in some way — as plans are always liable to do. Our loss was 290, more than half of

it in Gracie's brigade. This virtually ended the fighting of the campaign, in which our entire losses were 198 killed, 850 wounded, 248 missing,— total, 1296. Burnside's losses were 92 killed, 393 wounded, and 207 missing,— total, 692.— E. P. A.

The Union force at Bean's Station consisted of 4000 cavalry, under General Shackelford, who led the advance of a column commanded by General Parke. Parke, with the infantry, was approaching, and sent a division against Martin's cavalry, preventing the flank movement here referred to as having miscarried.— EDITORS.

expedities, and alarms enough to destroy most of the comfort of winter-quarters. ☆

In the latter part of March we moved back to Bristol, and in April General Lee sent for us to rejoin him by rail. Reaching Gordonsville on the

☆ We had some of our foraging wagons captured and men killed by the "bushwhackers." The latter were supposed to be guerrilla troops in the Federal service

22d of April, we were once more with the Army of Northern Virginia, just twelve days before it entered the Wilderness and began the death-grapple that was only to end, after eleven months of daily fighting, at Appomattox.

recruited among the people of that section whose sympathies were anti-Confederate. They seldom fought, but they cut off small parties and took no prisoners.— E. P. A.

KNOXVILLE IN 1870. FROM A WATER-COLOR SKETCH.

THE OPPOSING FORCES AT KNOXVILLE, TENN.
November 17th–December 4th, 1863.

For much of the information contained in this list and in similar lists to follow, the editors are indebted (in advance of the publication of the "Official Records") to Brigadier-General Richard C. Drum, Adjutant-General of the Army. K stands for killed; w for wounded; m w for mortally wounded; m for captured or missing; c for captured.

THE UNION ARMY.

ARMY OF THE OHIO — Major-General Ambrose E. Burnside.

NINTH ARMY CORPS, Brig.-Gen. Robert B. Potter. *Escort:* 6th Ind. Cav. (4 co's), Col. James Biddle. Loss: k, 1; w, 1; m, 1 = 3.
FIRST DIVISION, Brig.-Gen. Edward Ferrero.
First Brigade, Col. David Morrison: 36th Mass., Maj. William F. Draper; 8th Mich., Lieut.-Col. Ralph Ely; 79th N. Y., Capt. William S. Montgomery; 45th Pa., Lieut.-Col. Francis M. Hills. Brigade loss: k, 4; w, 19; m, 6 = 29. *Second Brigade,* Col. Benjamin C. Christ: 29th Mass., Col. Ebenezer W. Peirce; 27th Mich., Maj. William B. Wright; 46th N. Y., Capt. Alphons Serieri; 50th Pa., Maj. Edward Overton, Jr. Brigade loss: k, 15; w, 25; m, 24 = 64. *Third Brigade,* Col. William Humphrey: 2d Mich., Maj. Cornelius Byington (m w); Capt. John C. Ruehl; 17th Mich., Lieut.-Col. Lorin L. Comstock (k), Capt. Frederick W. Swift; 20th Mich., Maj. Byron M. Cutcheon; 100th Pa., Lieut.-Col. Matthew M. Dawson. Brigade loss: k, 18; w, 102; m, 46 = 166. *Artillery:* 34th N. Y., Capt. Jacob Roemer; D, 1st R. I., Capt. William W. Buckley. Artillery loss: w, 2.
SECOND DIVISION, Col. John F. Hartranft.
First Brigade, Col. Joshua K. Sigfried: 2d Md., Col. Thomas B. Allard; 21st Mass., Lieut.-Col. George P. Hawkes; 48th Pa., Maj. Joseph A. Gilmour. Brigade loss: k, 5; w, 27; m, 32 = 64. *Second Brigade,* Lieut.-Col. Edwin Schall: 35th Mass., Maj. Nathaniel Wales; 11th N. H., Capt. Leander W. Cogswell; 51st Pa., Maj. William J. Bolton. Brigade loss: k, 4; w, 7; m, 3 = 14.

UNATTACHED: E, 2d U. S. Art'y, Lieut. Samuel N. Benjamin.
TWENTY-THIRD ARMY CORPS, Brig.-Gen. Mahlon D. Manson.
General Headquarters: McLaughlin's Ohio Squadron Cav., Maj. Richard Rice; Eng. Battalion, Capt. O. S. McClure.
SECOND DIVISION, Brig.-Gen. Julius White. Staff loss: m, 2.
Second Brigade, Col. Marshall W. Chapin: 107th Ill., Lieut.-Col. Francis H. Lowry; 13th Ky., Col. William E. Hobson; 23d Mich., Maj. William W. Wheeler; 111th Ohio, Maj. Isaac R. Sherwood; Ill. Battery, Capt. Edward C. Henshaw. Brigade loss: w, 13; m, 4 = 17.
THIRD DIVISION, Brig.-Gen. Milo S. Hascall.
First Brigade, Col. James W. Reilly: 44th Ohio, Maj. Alpheus S. Moore; 100th Ohio, Col. Patrick S. Slevin; 104th Ohio, Lieut.-Col. Oscar W. Sterl; D, 1st Ohio Art'y, Lieut. William H. Pease. Brigade loss: k, 2; w, 15; m, 7 = 24. *Second Brigade,* Col. Daniel Cameron: 65th Ill., Lieut.-Col. William S. Stewart; 24th Ky., Col. John S. Hunt; 103d Ohio, Capt. John T. Philpot; Ind. Battery, Capt. Hubbard T. Thomas. Brigade loss: k, 9; w, 97; m, 2 = 108.
RESERVE ARTILLERY, Capt. Andrew J. Konkle: 24th Ind., Capt. Joseph A. Sims; 19th Ohio, Capt. Joseph C. Shields.
Provisional Brigade, Col. William A. Hoskins: 12th

Ky., Maj. Joseph M. Owens; 8th Tenn., Col. Felix A. Reeve. *Tennessee Brigade*, Col. John S. Casement.

CAVALRY CORPS, Brig.-Gen. James M. Shackelford. FIRST DIVISION, Brig.-Gen. William P. Sanders (m w), Col. Frank Wolford. Staff loss: m w, 1.

First Brigade, Col. Frank Wolford, Lieut.-Col. Silas Adams: 1st Ky., Lieut.-Col. Silas Adams; 11th Ky., ———; 12th Ky., ———; Law's Howitzer Battery,———. Brigade loss: k, 5; w, 9; m, 10 = 24. *Second Brigade*, Lieut.-Col. Emery S. Bond: 112th Ill. (mounted infantry), Maj. Tristram T. Dow; 8th Mich.,———; 45th Ohio (mounted infantry),———; 15th Ind. Battery,———. Brigade loss: k, 25; w, 63; m, 64 = 152. *Third Brigade*,

Col. Charles D. Pennebaker: 11th Ky., Col. S. Palace Love; 27th Ky., Lieut.-Col. John H. Ward. Brigade loss: k, 4; w, 12; m, 1 = 17.

SECOND DIVISION.

First Brigade, Col. Israel Garrard: 2d Ohio, Lieut.-Col. George A. Purington; 7th Ohio, ———; 2d Tenn. (infantry), ———. Brigade loss: m, 5. Total Union loss: killed 92, wounded 394, captured or missing, 207 = 693.

In his official report General Burnside says: "Our force at this time [commencement of the siege] in Knoxville was about 12,000 effective men, exclusive of the new recruits of loyal Tennesseeans."

THE CONFEDERATE ARMY.

Lieut.-Gen. James Longstreet. Staff loss: w, 1.

McLAWS'S DIVISION, Maj.-Gen. Lafayette McLaws.

Kershaws's Brigade, Brig.-Gen. Joseph B. Kershaw: 2d S. C., Col. John D. Kennedy (w), Lieut.-Col. F. Gaillard; 3d S. C., Col. James D. Nance; 7th S. C., Capt. E. J. Goggans; 8th S. C., Col. J. W. Henagan, Capt. D. McIntyre; 15th S. C., Maj. William M. Gist (k), Capt. J. B. Davis; 3d S. C. Battalion, Lieut.-Col. W. G. Rice. Brigade loss: k, 19; w, 116; m, 3 = 138. *Wofford's Brigade*, Col. S. Z. Ruff (k), Lieut.-Col. N. L. Hutchins, Jr.: 16th Ga., Lieut.-Col. Henry P. Thomas (k); 18th Ga., Capt. John A. Crawford; 24th Ga., Capt. N. J. Dortch; Cobb's (Ga.) Legion, Maj. William D. Conyers; Phillips (Ga.) Legion, Maj. Joseph Hamilton (w); 3d Ga. Battalion Sharp-shooters, Lieut.-Col. N. L. Hutchins, Jr. Brigade loss: k, 48; w, 121; m, 81 = 250. *Humphreys's Brigade*, Brig.-Gen. Benjamin G. Humphreys: 13th Miss., Col. Kennon McElroy (k), Maj. G. L. Donald; 17th Miss., Lieut.-Col. John C. Fiser (w); 18th Miss., Col. Thomas M. Griffin; 21st Miss., Col. W. L. Brandon. Brigade loss: k, 21; w, 105; m, 56 = 182. *Bryan's Brigade*, Brig.-Gen. Goode Bryan: 10th Ga., Lieut.-Col. Willis C. Holt; 50th Ga., Col. P. McGlashan; 51st Ga., Col. E. Ball; 53d Ga., Col. James P. Simms (w). Brigade loss: k, 27; w, 121; m, 64 = 212.

HOOD'S DIVISION, Brig.-Gen. Micah Jenkins.

Jenkins's Brigade, Col. John Bratton: 1st S. C., Col. F. W. Kilpatrick; 2d S. C. Rifles, Col. Thomas Thomson; 5th S. C., Col. A. Coward; 6th S. C.———; Hampton (S. C.) Legion, Col. M. W. Gary; Palmetto (S. C.) Sharp-shooters, Col. Joseph Walker. Brigade loss: k, 22; w, 109; m, 5 = 136. *Robertson's Brigade*, Brig.-Gen. Jerome B. Robertson: 3d Ark., Col. Van H. Manning; 1st Tex., Col. A. T. Rainey; 4th Tex., Col. J. C. G. Key; 5th Tex., Col. R. M. Powell. Brigade loss: k, 9; w, 18; m, 6 = 33. *Law's Brigade*, Brig.-Gen. E. McIver Law: 4th Ala., Col. P. D. Bowles; 15th Ala., Col. W. C. Oates; 44th Ala., Col. W. F. Perry; 47th Ala., Col. M. J. Bulger; 48th Ala., Col. James L. Sheffield. Brigade loss: k, 15; w, 69; m, 8 = 92. *Anderson's Brigade*, Brig.-Gen. G. T. Anderson: 7th Ga., Col. W. W. White; 8th Ga., Col. John R. Towers; 9th Ga., Col. Benjamin Beck; 11th Ga., Col. F. H. Little; 59th Ga., Col. Jack Brown. Brigade loss: k, 36; w, 186; m, 25 = 247. *Benning's Brigade*, Brig.-Gen. Henry L. Benning: 2d Ga., Col. E. M. Butt; 15th Ga., Col. D. M. Du Bose; 17th Ga., Col. Wesley C. Hodges; 20th Ga., Col. J. D. Waddell. Brigade loss: k, 1; w, 5 = 6.

ARTILLERY, Col. E. P. Alexander.

Leyden's Battalion, Maj. A. Leyden: Ga. Battery, Capt. Tyler M. Peeples; Ga. Battery, Capt. A. M. Wolihin; Ga. Battery, Capt. B. W. York. *Alexander's Battalion*, Maj. Frank Huger: La. Battery, Capt. G. V. Moody; Va. Battery, Capt. W. W. Fickling; Va. Battery, Capt. Tyler C. Jordan; Va. Battery, Capt. William W. Parker; Va. Battery, Capt. Osmond B. Taylor; Va. Battery, Capt. Pichigru Woolfolk, Jr. Artillery loss: k, 2; w, 2 = 4.

BUCKNER'S DIVISION, ☆ Brig.-Gen. Bushrod R. Johnson.

Gracie's Brigade, Brig.-Gen. Archibald Gracie, Jr.: 41st Ala., Lieut.-Col. T. G. Trimmier; 43d Ala., Col. Y. M. Moody; 59th Ala., Lieut.-Col. J. D. McLennan; 60th Ala., Col. J. W. A. Sanford. Brigade loss: k, 1; w, 1 = 2. *Johnson's Brigade*, Col. John S. Fulton: 17th and 23d Tenn., Lieut.-Col. W. W. Floyd; 25th and 44th Tenn., Lieut.-Col. J. L. McEwen, Jr.; 63d Tenn., Maj. J. A. Aiken. Brigade loss: k, 2; w, 19 = 21.

CAVALRY CORPS, Maj.-Gen. Joseph Wheeler, Maj.-Gen. William T. Martin.

Division commanders: Maj.-Gen. William T. Martin, Brig.-Gen's F. C. Armstrong and John T. Morgan. *Brigade commanders:* Colonels Thomas Harrison, A. A. Russell, C. C. Crews, and George G. Dibrell. *Troops:* Parts of 4th, 8th, 9th, and 11th Tenn., 1st, 2d, 3d, 4th, and 6th Ga., 1st, 3d, 4th, 7th, and 51st Ala., 3d Ark., 8th and 11th Tex., and 1st and 8th Confederate regiments, and Wiggins's Battery. Cavalry loss (estimated): k, w and m, 200.

RANSOM'S CAVALRY. ⸗

Jones's Brigade, Brig.-Gen. William E. Jones: 8th Va., Col. James M. Corns; 21st Va.,———; 27th Va. Battalion, ———; 34th Va. Battalion, Col. V. A. Witcher; 36th Va. Battalion,———; 27th Va. Battalion,———. *Giltner's Brigade*, Col. H. L. Giltner: 16th Ga. Battalion, Maj. E. Y. Clark; 4th Ky., Maj. N. Parker; 10th Ky., Lieut.-Col. Edwin Trimble; 1st Tenn., Col. James E. Carter; 64th Va., Col. Campbell Slemp; Va. Battery, Capt. William N. Lowry.

The total Confederate loss (minus the cavalry, not reported) was 182 killed, 768 wounded, and 192 captured or missing = 1142. The loss in the cavalry is estimated at 250.

The effective strength of the forces under Longstreet's command probably numbered 20,000.

☆ Joined November 26th-28th.

⸗ Joined November 27th-28th.

END OF VOLUME III.

www.ingramcontent.com/pod-product-compliance
Lightning Source LLC
Chambersburg PA
CBHW081640040426

42449CB00014B/3402